NOTHING LIKE THE WOODEN HORSE

Tom Kelly

Red Squirrel Press

First published in the U.K. in 2009
by Red Squirrel Press

PO BOX 219 MORPETH NE61 9AU
www.redsquirrelpress.com

Cover design by Adam Heslop and The Customs House

ISBN 978-1-906700-11-9

Printed in the U.K. by Athenaeum Press Ltd.
Gateshead, Tyne & Wear

NOTHING LIKE THE WOODEN HORSE
Tom Kelly

The Jarrow born poet and playwright has had many productions at the Customs House, South Shields. He has worked with John Miles on three staged musicals at the Customs House, (*The Machine Gunners, Tom & Catherine & Dan Dare*) and with Alan Price, on *Kelly*, a musical documentary and the subject of a BBC Arena Programme, "There won't be a dry eye in the house," Lord Mountbatten.

"his writing strikes a chord with local audiences... even though his themes may be universal... the settings and characters are very Tyneside." The British Theatre Guide.

"Tom Kelly provides pathos and humour as John Sullivan does in the best of *Fools and Horses*" Evening Chronicle.

In 2007 he had a poetry collection *The Wrong Jarrow* published by Smokestack Books, "Kelly writes with an uncomfortable rawness and directness... an honesty we are much in need of." Matt Simpson, Critical Survey.
"Jarrow is in his bones... there is heartache and pain in these poems." Jim Burns, Ambit.

In 2008 his poetry collection *Dreamers in a Cold Climate* was published by Red Squirrel, "A beautiful elegy to work and the industrial working class," Morning Star.

His most recent collection *Love-Lines* has just been published by Red Squirrel and he has just completed a documentary film with South Shields filmmaker, Gary Wilkinson, *Little Ireland* which examines the impact of the Irish in Jarrow.

Nothing Like The Wooden Horse was first produced by the Customs House, Mill Dam, South Shields on 18th March 2009

The cast:

Tommy Henderson	**Donald McBride**
Wayne Robson	**Michael Imerson**
Director	**Jackie Fielding**
Designer	**Simon Henderson**
Production Manager	**Alison Hickman**
Lights/Sound	**Chris Allen, Nick Morrison**
Stage Manager	**Martin Hogg**

The action of the play takes place in Jarrow, Norway, Poland, Germany and Baghdad between 1939 and 2008.

Introduction

Plays change. *Nothing Like The Wooden Horse* is being published on the day rehearsals begin. It will take on a new life: the cast, director and writer will question everything and a play will emerge, different from the text being printed today.

Having said that, this is the play I have lived with over the past year and what you now have is the re-worked version after the director, Jackie Fielding, began to ask questions of me, which began with, 'Why?'

The play's origins are in part my dad's experiences as a Prisoner of War in Germany during the Second World War. Dad died in 1995 but thankfully I recorded a conversation with him not long before his death.

What I am trying to capture in *Nothing Like The Wooden Horse* is the impact of war on two working class men. What were their hopes when they joined the army? What was the reality? What did they endure? I was aware, through my dad, of the horrors of war.
I dedicate this play to my dad Tommy Kelly.

I would like to acknowledge the tremendous support of the *Nothing Like The Wooden Horse* director Jackie Fielding; Ray Spencer and everyone at the wonderful Customs House, South Shields and Sheila Wakefield of Red Squirrel Press.

Tom Kelly
February 2009

Act One

Jarrow, South Tyneside, 2008.

The Living Room of Tommy Henderson's council bungalow. The room is neat: a sideboard with family photographs, small ornaments and a settee where he sits holding an envelope in front of a coffee table with his medals and photographs of Tommy and Grandson Wayne.

Tommy pushes the envelope to one side as Wayne enters with a carrier bag containing cans of lager.

TOMMY   Aa thought you weren't going ti' bother. Aa was half-asleep. It's nearlee past me bed-time. Have ye been for aa pint?

WAYNE   No.

TOMMY   *Indicating cans.* Aa see ye've got wa rations. Aa've still got that bottle of champagne you and Tracey gave me for me birthday, wi could open that.

WAYNE   No.

TOMMY   What time de ye leave tommorra?

WAYNE   First thing.

TOMMY   With aa heavy bloody heart.

WAYNE   Yes.

TOMMY   By th' time aa'm listening ti th' match ye'll be back in ya barracks. It's aa six pointer. De ye think Wayne?

WAYNE   Yes.

TOMMY   Aa tell ye what forget th' cans and open that bottle of champagne.

Wayne picking up envelope.

WAYNE	What's this?
TOMMY	It's from the hospital. It's nowt.
WAYNE	The hospital?
TOMMY	Aa had some tests.
WAYNE	You don't get tests for nothing.
TOMMY	Aa've had aa bit bother with me chest.
WAYNE	So you're all right now?
TOMMY	Champion.
WAYNE	Good.

TOMMY *Reading from photograph.*
Marienberg, Germany, P.O.W. Camp Number 409.
Stalag XXB. *To Wayne.* Stalag camps were for 'other ranks'. Like me. Th' had camps for officers called Oflags. Officers didn't work. We did.

WAYNE Right.

TOMMY Th' camps wor nothing like th' film, 'The Wooden Horse!' It was about aa Oflag prisoner of war camp in Germany. Came out after th' war. Officers with stiff-upper lips wor always trying ti escape. *Posh officer voice.* "I say old chaps de ye fancy aa spot of tunnel digging?" It was nowt like th' camps aa was in. Aa bloody hate that film.

WAYNE You want to see the camps I've been working in.

TOMMY At least you're th' bloody guard.

WAYNE I don't want to go back.

TOMMY Your uncle went AWOL in th' Second World War. Me da took him right back ti his barracks. By th' time da got home th' army police were knocking our door down!

WAYNE   What happened?

TOMMY   Caught him in th' bar of the 'Robin Hood.' Never was th'
brightest. Instead of takin' him back to his regiment, they sent him ti India.

WAYNE   They always get you.

TOMMY   Once ye sign-up. What's th' matter wi' you? Ya full of
hell about somethin.'

WAYNE   Everything.

TOMMY   Ah'm aa going ti find out?
Tommy looking at a photograph.
               Aa was on th' dole when aa signed-up in th' Summer of
1939. Me and me mates went ti' Newcastle, had aa bloody good drink an' by
th' time aa got back home aa was in th' Green Howards! Me father cried
when aa told him.

WAYNE   My mother didn't.

TOMMY   That's what you think. She broke her bloody heart.

WAYNE   Did she? Why?

TOMMY   She didn't want ya arse shot off. Look what's happened
to your mates. Ya mother and ya Granny never let me talk about th' army.

WAYNE   But you did.

TOMMY   Aa never went on about it. Now and again mebbe.

WAYNE   Not enough for me. *Indicating.* I used to love sneaking a
look at these medals and photos. Imagine myself in uniform. I didn't really
know what being a soldier meant.

TOMMY   Aa could have told ye'.

WAYNE   By not saying you made it more exciting. Like a big secret. You know what that does?

TOMMY   Makes ye full of hell?

WAYNE   You want it more.

Wayne, eighteen, with his mother.

WAYNE   Mam I've always wanted to join the army. I'm eighteen now. Northern Ireland's dead quiet. They use them rubber bullets that bounce off you.
You know the papers and telly exaggerate. I'll get a trade in the army. I'm wasting my time round here: stacking shelves in a supermarket! The boredom's killing me. What will I do for the rest of me life? Crap jobs. It's the right thing to do. Trust me. Anyway it's too late to stop us. Tracey thinks it's a good idea. I'm going.

TOMMY   Aa didn't mean ti encourage ye.

WAYNE   You did. Don't forget that.

TOMMY   You're like me.

WAYNE   A pain in the arse.

TOMMY   Aa've had ti keep things ti mesel'. You're th' same.

WAYNE   I'm not!

TOMMY   Ya Granny cried at th' drop of a hat. She'd say, "aa'll kill ya if you talk about th' war," Since she died aa've had more time t' dwell on things. *Picking up a can.* Do ye want one?

Tommy looking at a photograph of Wayne in uniform.

TOMMY   When aa saw you in your uniform for th' first time it was like seeing meself. Same age as you. Young and daft.
Tommy, as young man, looking to an upstairs window.

TOMMY   Ma you know who it is! Tommy, ya son. Been ti th'bar
with th' lads. Don't ignore me, just cos aa've had aa drink. Aa can see ya
behind th' curtains. Ye know it's me.
Aa've signed-up for th' Green Howard's. Aa go for training first then off ti
fight Jerry. Th' army'll be great. Aa'll see th' world.
To Wayne. Then she opened th' door and cracked me on th' head. She didn't
cry.

WAYNE   My mother cried and didn't tell me.

TOMMY   She should have. Th' say there's nothing wrong with
saying how ye feel. Sometimes you've just got to.

WAYNE   Do you reckon?

TOMMY   Aa don't know. But ye can't show it. Ya mates would
have ya life.

WAYNE   You've got to keep it inside. All the things you want to
talk about. I felt sorry for the Iraqi prisoners.

TOMMY   Being aa prisoner changes ye. Aal aa wanted ti do was
live another day. Aa did things aa would never do: ye couldn't show th'
guards how ye felt.

WAYNE   What kept you going?

TOMMY   Geordie. We'd sit on our bunks and pick lice off each
other like animals in cages.

WAYNE   Trapped.

TOMMY   Day and night living in th' same clothes.

WAYNE   Half our army gear was useless! Remember when
Granny sent me a pair of boots? The ones they gave us melted!

TOMMY   She went to th' town by herself, determined ti do something for her grandbairn. Paid aa fortune for th' buggers. She was proud as punch when she posted them to ye just like th' Red Cross parcels we used ti get, th' kept us going.

WAYNE   I lived for emails and calls from Tracey. And your letters with stories you'd cut out the paper, they helped me cope.

TOMMY   *Indicating photograph.* That's Geordie. On me wedding day. He was best man. Great lad. We left Jarra high as bloody kites, went ti Richmond Barracks and finished wa training at Wetherby.
Then ti' France, th' Maginot Line. It was th' first time aa'd been out th' country. Three months on night patrols. After that we wor sent ti Rosyth in Scotland, th' kitted us out in fur boots and gloves.
Me and Geordie were on th' HMS Birmingham, in convoy, April, 1940, we wor part of th' Narvik campaign, not that we knew! Th' Germans had just invaded Norway.

Tommy and Wayne, as Geordie, April 1940, onboard HMS Birmingham.

SFX: Ship at sea.
Lights: temporary lightning strung throughout the ship.

WAYNE   *As Geordie.* Tommy di' ye knaa where wa goin?

TOMMY   *Indicating uniform.* Geordie it'll not be India with us dressed like polar bears.

WAYNE   *As Geordie.* Ye've got aa point. Nevva thought o' that.

TOMMY   *Indicating O.S.* Aa sailor said, "Wa headin' for colder waters."

WAYNE   *As Geordie.* As long as aa don't hav' ti swim.

TOMMY   Why's that?

WAYNE   *As Geordie.* Aa cannit!

TOMMY   *Indicating O.S.* That sailor told us waa goin' ti Norway.

WAYNE   *As Geordie.* Near India?

SFX: Torpedo explosion.
Tommy and Geordie are thrown violently around lighting flickers out and
returns as previously.

WAYNE   *As Geordie.* What de ye reckon that was?

TOMMY   Aa torpedo that got aa bit too close but we'll be aal reet.

WAYNE   *As Geordie.* How's that?

TOMMY   Aa torpedo can nevva sink aa ship with two daft
Geordies onboard.

WAYNE   *As Geordie.* Just as well wa here.

TOMMY   Did aa tell ya what Paddy Devlin said ti me, mind he'd
had aa canny drink. *Irish voice.* "Young Tommy, show me the door and I'll
find the house meself". Th' Irishmen in th' lodging houses share th' same
bed.

WAYNE   *As Geordie.* Aa share with me three brothers.

TOMMY   Th' one on night shift sleeps during th' day and th' one
on day shift sleeps in th' same bed at night...

WAYNE   *As Geordie.* Sometimes aa hav ti share with aa bed
wetter. Aa make sure aa sleep in th' shallow end.

TOMMY   Wi' bugs for company. Aa've seen me ma clean and
scrub our house from top ti' bottom and th' bugs go next door!

WAYNE   *As Geordie.* Aa've sat and squashed them many aa night.
Th' walls are wick with them.

TOMMY   Like th' Means Test Men. They're everywhere. Aalways at ye. Workin' with tha' police ti keep ya down. Me da says, "Its aa police state". Aa'd take that now. It's something aa knaa. Wa in aa different world. Like our officers.

WAYNE   *As Geordie.* Aa knaa what ye mean! Aa can't understand aa word tha saying.

TOMMY   One of them said, "What's your name Private?" Aa said, "Private Thomas Henderson. Sir! Aa was born an bred in Jarra. Joined th' Green Howards. Sir. Aa was sent ti' Richmond. Did me training at Wetherby. Then ti th Maginot Line. And now ah'm here. Sir! He saluted and nevvor said aa word. Aa could tell he didn't know what aa'd said.

WAYNE   *As Geordie.* Th' couldn't understand me at aal! Aa can talk propaa, its them buggas that taalk foreign. Ah'm glad you're heor Tommy. Ye knaa what's happenin'. Aa haven't aa clue.

They sway slowly from side-to-side.

WAYNE   *As Geordie.* Aa wi' nearlee there?

TOMMY   Wa nearlee there.

WAYNE   *As Geordie.* Where's that?

TOMMY   Norway! And it'll be bloody caad.

SFX: Bomb explosions and gunfire.
Lights: flares on sea at night.
Tommy and Geordie walk forward into the sea, rifles held above their heads.

TOMMY   Aa knaa ye can't swim Geordie... ah'm behind ye... *Indicating.* That's reet, keep ya rifle above ya heed!

WAYNE   *As Geordie.* It's so caad, aa canna get me breath.

TOMMY   Th' hairs up me nose are cracklin.'

WAYNE   *As Geordie.* Th' waatta's freezin.'

SFX: Gunfire above and around them.
A searchlight trawls the sea.

TOMMY   Jerry's waiting for us Geordie...

WAYNE   *As Geordie.* Gan canny Tommy…

TOMMY   *Indicating to Geordie.* Follow that lot…

WAYNE   *As Geordie.* Ah'm with you bonny lad!

Tommy and Wayne now.

Tommy picks up the book 'Denmark and Norway 1940.'

TOMMY   *Indicating book.* Ya mam bought this for me. It's like aa
diary of me life at th' time. *Reading.* "April 1940: Th' Narvik campaign…
Hitler's boldest operation." *Stops reading and to Wayne.* Was aa disaster!
We wor hammered. Lost most of our battalion.
Norwegian ski-troopers took us to aa farm and we slept with th' cattle under
th' house. Twenty of us, that's all that wor left. All th' officers had been
killed.
We headed for Sweden, it was aa neutral country. Aa was starving, me
tongue like leather, with sucking snow. We went from house ti' house.
Norwegian peasants hid us. Th' could have been shot for helping.
Ye had ti have eyes up your arse. Didn't know who ye could trust. Frozen ti
th' bone. We met this Norwegian. Seemed like aa great bloke. Aa thought,
thank God some bugger's helping.
He was going ti get us into Sweden, my arse! Th' 'great bloke' was aa
Quisling. Walked us into aa trap. Th' Germans shouted, "Halt".
And that was me, aa prisoner of war.

WAYNE   You feel like a prisoner even though you're the one
shouting. *To prisoners.* "Move or you'll get my shiny boot right up your
hole. Don't start. Stop bloody chanting! Stop staring at me. You're the
prisoner mate. Sit down and shut up. *Indicating.* Shit there".
To Tommy The smell was enough to make you vote Tory.

TOMMY   We had aa guard, we called him 'Scarface'. Not ti his face! Vicious bastard. One of me mates was Jewish. 'Scarface' suspected, an' every chance he'd be at him. One day he kicked th' Jewish lad and aa grabbed his rifle.

To Scarface. "Leave him alone. Ye bastard. Get off him".

To Wayne. He tuk us to the Camp commandant. Aa could have got aa real bollocking. Anyway aa'd noticed 'Scarface' didn't hav' his tunic buttoned-up properly and his cap badge was missing. Aa said he was aa disgrace. Me and th' Jewish lad stood erect.

Th' Commandant looked at th' three of us then told us ti leave. We got away with it! Aa thought 'Scarface' would kill us but he kept his distance. If he saw ye wor weak he'd be on ya bones.

WAYNE   I could have killed one of the prisoners. He kept crying and throwing his hands in the air. His chanting was doing my head in.

Wayne in an Iraqi Prison, 2004.

WAYNE   *To prisoners.* Listen you're the prisoners.

Do... as... I... say. Shut up! *Indicating.* Against... the... wall. Stand. Stand! No, don't sit.

Demonstrating to Iraqi prisoners, standing to attention against the wall.

To Dave. Dave it's not a joke. I'm not bloody laughing.

That's right, like Dave. No! There's no need to salute! They'll do the same as you Dave. You've got them lying on the bloody floor! *To Prisoners.* Don't laugh at me! You, stop that bloody chanting.

Losing control.

What you saying? 'Wa alikum salaam, Wa alikum salaam...'

Screaming into Habib's face.

Are you praying against me? Stop that bloody, 'Wa alikum salaam.'

Tommy and Wayne now.

WAYNE   I pulled the gun. That shut him up. I had power. The gun in my hand. Couldn't stand having that control. Was I getting off on it? It makes you do things. It's still going round in my head. You shouldn't have that power.

TOMMY   Like 'Scarface'.

WAYNE   I still see that prisoner, Habib, hear him, I saw… did…
some things… dream about them.

TOMMY   Ah'm th' same, sixty years later. At least aa don't wake
anybody up now, ya Granny went years without aa good nights sleep.
After our war, ye never had any of ya 'psychological treatment..'

WAYNE   They call them 'de-briefs' to make sure you're alright to
go back again. They can't do anything with the lads that go AWOL. Or the
suicides.

TOMMY   It was straight back ti Civvy Street: get yourself aa job,
be glad ya home. Aa couldn't stay in th' house. Aa'd come out in aa cold
sweat if aa door slammed. Aa closed me eyes an it would start, th' pictures
of all th' things aa'd been through. Aa dreamed bugs wor burying
themselves into me body.
Ya Granny tried to help me when aa first came out th' army. She'd say,
"Have aa early night." But aa didn't want ti go ti bed. Th' walls closed in as
soon as aa shut me eyes. Aa was back in th' camps: smelt th' straw on me
bunk, bugs crawling over me body. Aa'd throw th' blankets off and dive out
of bed.
Aa tried ti throttle ya Granny one night. Grabbed aa handful of hair. We wor
scrabbling on th' floor when aa woke up. Wouldn't hurt her for th' world.
Aa cried me heart out. We had some black days an nights. Aa always have
aa light on in th' bedroom, it doesn't stop th' past battering in.
Aa'd fall asleep in front of th' fire, wake up shouting and sweating like aa
bloody pig.

WAYNE   I'm the same. The first time Tracey thought I'd pissed
meself.

TOMMY   Is that when she started wearing aa sowester in bed?

WAYNE   She didn't mind me getting up during the night with the
bairn, he kept me company. I'd give him his bottle, sit there and forget all
the stuff, burning a bloody hole in my head.

TOMMY   At half-three in th' morning, th' dead hours.

WAYNE   We could have sat side-by-side. She's used to me going in the spare room now.

Tommy opens a can of lager.

WAYNE   Give us a can. I'm bloody sweating.

TOMMY   Aa'll hav ti wear Tracey's sowester.

WAYNE   That's how it's got me.

TOMMY   Ye get over it, nae bother at all. Give it another sixty years and ye'll be fine.

WAYNE   As long as you can manage with no legs. And that's not counting what it does to your head.

TOMMY   There was aa lad aa knew, after th' war, he couldn't stop screaming in th' street. Bairns would shout after him, he'd chase them until th' Polis picked him up. Hung hissel'. Used his regimental tie.

WAYNE   I've been thinking about leaving the army, be a full-time dad.

TOMMY   Get out in one piece, before ye end up like Dave.

WAYNE   Our first tour in Iraq was hard but I was with a great bunch of lads. Saw Sadam's statue fall.
Dave kept saying, "We'll clear this place up, no bother. Where's their crack Republican Guard? The Iraqis want us here. Glad of us. Money for old rope Wayne."
The second tour was murder. Lads killed every day, roadside bombs and the barracks attacked. You see all the stuff on the television but we can't switch it off. Dave was sitting in the front of the Land Rover. I can see him, hear the engine.

SFX: Land Rover engine revving up.

WAYNE   He shouted, "Come on Wayne! You'll be late for your own funeral."
In action I gave him the V's. And shouted, "Give your mouth a break Dave."
He looked at the rest of the lads and in this daft girlie voice said, "Ohh Wayne's touchy today!"   Then he laughed and shouted, "Right lads, next stop the Pier Head!"

SFX: Explosion: a roadside bomb, flashing lights and flames from the Land Rover.
Wayne runs forward in action.

WAYNE   I held him close and screamed, "No! You'll make it, come on Dave."
He shouted, "No!" It was his twenty-first birthday.

TOMMY   That's the first time ye've told me th' whole story.

WAYNE   Dave's wife left him. Said she couldn't stand looking at his amputated legs and scars all over his body.
He had forty-percent burns. He said, "I don't know why I'm living Wayne". I didn't have an answer.

TOMMY   And ye never forget. Geordie an' me wor queuing for soup in Limburg, one of th' camps in Poland. It was like th' united nations, POW's from aal over Europe. We wor at th' back. God aa was clammin!

Linberg POW Camp, Poland, 1942.

Tommy and Wayne, as Geordie, meal-time.

TOMMY   *Looking at queue.* Geordie, aa you thinkin' what ah'm
thinking?

WAYNE   *As Geordie.* It's aa long queue.

TOMMY   If wi don't eat we've had it.

WAYNE   *As Geordie.* Th'll not let us go ti th' front, we're aal in th' same boat. They've been queuing for ages.

TOMMY   Aa've got aa can of hot water.

WAYNE   *As Geordie.* Be careful ye might scald somebody.

TOMMY   That's th' idea!

Tommy begins to walk to the front of the queue.

TOMMY   Ah'm going ti th' front.

Wayne, as Geordie, follows Tommy.

WAYNE   *As Geordie.* They'll not like it.

TOMMY   When aa throw th' hot waata grab ya fill of th' soup.

WAYNE   *As Geordie.* Th' water's hot! You'll scald them.

TOMMY   Do as aa say.

WAYNE   *As Geordie.* Right Tommy.

Tommy throws the hot water at the other P.O.W's.

SFX: Men screaming.
Wayne, as Geordie, quickly fills a tin with soup.

Tommy and Wayne now.

TOMMY   Aa wasn't proud of that. Aa had ti do it: if ya don't eat ya
don't live.

WAYNE   Is that why you have your arm round the plate when
you're eating?

TOMMY   Protecting me food aa suppose? Ye knaa aa aalways feel
hungry. Ye had to hang onto everything and th' lads round me weren't even
th' enemy.

WAYNE   In Iraq you don't know your enemies. You can't trust anybody. You give sweets to bairns in the street and they throw stones at you. Suicide bombers, walking into cafés and markets full of women and bairns.

TOMMY   Th' reckon suicide bombers say they're going somewhere better, mebbe th' can't think of anywhere worse.

WAYNE   You start thinking everybody's a bomber, your eyes start to twitch.

TOMMY   When some buggers nice ti ye you don't know what ti do. After aa was captured aa had this dead feeling in me stomach. Thought everybody had forgot us. Aa'd look at mesel, skin and bone, hands like bell metal, wi' working every minute God sent. Time was dead. Aa started ti think aa'd nevvor get home. Th' Germans had us working on a Polish farm and aa spent me twenty-first birthday shovelling pig shit.
No "haav anotha pint", no "aal th' best son", no cards on th' mantelpiece. Aa was lost. Then th' Polish farmer found out it was me borthday. Gave me aa pair of rosary beads, asked me to sing, with his family.

Tommy on a Polish Farm, 1942.

Tommy Sings, 'Ave Maria'
                    Ave Maria
                    Gratia plena
                    Maria, gratia plena
                    Maria, gratia plena
                    Ave, ave dominus
                    Sominus tecum
                    Benedicta tu in mulieribus
                    Et benedictus
                    Et benedictus
                    Et benedictus fructus ventris
                    Ventris tuae, Jesus
                    Ave Maria

TOMMY   Me ma loves that. Thank ye for th' present and for inviting me inta ya home, it's lovelee, ye've made me feel wanted. *Looking around.* With ya famliee, aa've nevva seen me fatha and motha for two years.

Tommy and Wayne now.

TOMMY   Aa felt near me familee but it didn't last. Aa ended up in
hospital with eczema, th' Polish doctor pretended aa wasn't getting any
better so th' could keep me in. On Christmas Eve, all th' staff came round
with unleavened bread in their mouths, aa had to break off aa piece with me
mouth, this was aa Polish custom, aa sign of love.

WAYNE   You couldn't stay in hospital forever. You were still
trapped. Just like me, it's a DVD I can't switch off. I'm in the prison and it's
on constant replay. The other prisoners I could handle but Habib got under
my skin.
I'd shout, "Shut it Habib! I can't stand it any more. You've got my head
done in. Can't take it. No more praying for Habib. Pray for Wayne.
Wayne. Wayne."
I was losing it. I said, "Should I tell you what it's like for me? I joined the
Army to see the world. Get a future. Where do I end up? In a shitty cell in
Iraq."

TOMMY   Aa was only aa bairn mesel, bloody freezing, sometimes
aa thought aa'l not last another day.
Aa can see mesel, sixty of us in aa hut, bunks three high, if ya got aa bottom
bunk ye could hear th' rats under th' floorboards. Aa had aa straw mattress.
Ye'd go ti sleep with filth in ya mouth and wake up with th' bugger!
Aa thought me head's ganna explode. Cattle sheds that's what they wor. At
neet ye'd shit and piss there. Everybody round ye. 'Privacy?' Then th' bugs
wor havin' aa go at ye. Dreams wor worse. One night in th' toilet aa found
aa lad who'd hung himsel'.
He was French and had aa canny pair of snow boots. Aa went ti tell th'
French officer and by th' time aa got back some bugga had pinched his
boots! Aa thought, "He'll not miss them."
It was happening all th' time. Aa saw lads eat aa crow, so bloody hungry, aa
knaa how th' felt.
In Jarra, in th' Thirties, we wor starving but in th' camps it was worse. How
di' ye tell anybody? What de ye say? Aa don't know how aa survived.

WAYNE   I don't know if I will.
Wayne squeezes a can of lager.
Weak as piss.

TOMMY   *Looking at the can of lager.*
Ah'm not that struck on it either. You bought th' bugger.
If ya knew th' half of it ye wouldn't sign up.

WAYNE   Living with the shit. Dave with no legs and scarred for
life. Not that it matters now.

Tommy opens two cans of lager, hands one to Wayne, they sit and drink.

TOMMY   If ye wor upset, as aa bairn, ye'd say, "Granda, aa'll not
sleep with bad things in me head."

WAYNE   Don't start talking about going to Shields?

TOMMY   T' th' beach. Just you and me.

WAYNE   Yes.

TOMMY   Two peas in aa pod!

WAYNE   So you say.

TOMMY   Along the beach with a ball and a bag of sweets. You
loved ya sweets. Aa don't knaa how ye've got any teeth!

WAYNE   You give us them.

Tommy and Wayne on the beach at South Shields, 1986.

Wayne is 8 year old, Tommy 60.

SFX: Summer, sea and seagulls
They walk side-by-side, Wayne imitates Tommy's walk.

WAYNE   Granda, Granda, Granda!

TOMMY   That's me.

WAYNE   De ye like sweets?

TOMMY   Jelly babies, so aa can bite tha heads off.

WAYNE   Do ye do that as well?

TOMMY   Gob stoppers ye suck til there's nowt left...

WAYNE   Aa love doing that!

TOMMY   And them big squares of toffee sticking ti ya teeth and 'Pick and Mix' where ye get wine gums and them yella sherbet sweets...

WAYNE   They're me favourites.

TOMMY   Which ones?

WAYNE   All of them!

WAYNE   Granda!

TOMMY   That's me.

WAYNE   *Indicating.* The fisherman's left that fish.

TOMMY   *Looking down.* On th' rocks.

WAYNE   It'll not get back in the water.

TOMMY   Th' tide'll take it away.

WAYNE   It'll be dead.

TOMMY   Mebbe's.

WAYNE   *Moving forward.*
             Aa'll climb down onto the rocks... save it...
He begins to climb down to the rocks.

TOMMY   Stay where ye are!
Wayne picks up the fish and then lets it go.

WAYNE   *Shouting.* It's swimming away Granda, aa saved it.

TOMMY   *Holding Wayne.* Ya mam and ya Granny would kill me if
anything happened ti my little soldier.

Wayne starts to march like a soldier on parade but swings his arms together.

WAYNE   Look at me Granda!

TOMMY   Don't swing ya arms at th' same time!

Tommy instructing and demonstrating to Wayne.

TOMMY   *To Wayne.* Left, right, left, right....

Wayne begins to march correctly.

TOMMY   That's right. Halt. Right...

Wayne turns to the right.

TOMMY   No! Not, 'that right'. Aa mean correct. Now stand, 'At
Ease.'

*Wayne stands 'At Ease': legs slightly apart, rifle to one side, running down
his side, the butt of his rifle resting by his feet, with his head looking straight
ahead.*

WAYNE   Ah'm going to be aa soldier?

TOMMY   Aa hope ye nevvor have ti go ti war. Aa saw enough of it.
Aa was a prisoner of war.

Wayne salutes.

WAYNE   Did ye try ti escape Granda?

TOMMY   There was nowhere ti go. Aa couldn't speak German or Polish. Me British soldiers' uniform would have stood out in th' street. Aa'd have been aa dead easy, 'I Spy.' "I spy with my little eye something beginning with 'g'."

WAYNE   *Pointing at Tommy.* Granda!

TOMMY   Ye get it right every time. Here ye are.
               Hands Wayne a sweet.

WAYNE   *Without looking, puts the sweet straight into his mouth.* Me favourite! It's great today.

TOMMY   What's ya favourite day?

WAYNE   Today.

TOMMY   Saturday?

WAYNE   Any day when I'm with you Granda. You're great.

TOMMY   Do ye not miss ya da?

WAYNE   Never see him to miss him!
Wayne jumps up and down as they walk.
               Granda, Granda, Granda...

TOMMY   That's me.

WAYNE   *Runs and throws the ball in the air, looking to the sky.* Look how far I've thrown it. Right in the sky. *Indicating.* That dog's got it!

TOMMY   Ask forrit back.

WAYNE   What should aa say?

TOMMY   Don't worry it'll drop th' ball beside ya.
Watching, then indicating. Aa told ya. I'll throw it. It'll bring it back ti ye.
Tommy throws the ball, then watches as the dog chases the ball.
                    Throw aa ball and they'll run all day.

WAYNE   You're right Granda.
Wayne picks up the ball tentatively.
To Tommy.   It's full of slaaver.

TOMMY   Aa knaa aa few people like that.

Wayne throws the ball again, as the dog brings it back to him.

WAYNE   This is great! Never had aa dog. Can aa take it home?
Are we going to the Fair?

TOMMY   It'll be somebody's dog. Anyway there's nowt ye like at
th' Fair! Just them dodgems, pop, slot machines and that daft laughing
policeman.

WAYNE   I'm scared of him.

TOMMY   Aa don't want ye frightened!

WAYNE   I'm not ...*that*... frightened. *Wayne indicating.* There's
the Fair Granda!

TOMMY   Aa love th' Fair. Ya Granny doesn't. Candy floss. Slot
machines. Th' waltzer.

SFX: Music from waltzer, 'Blue Suede Shoes.'

WAYNE   Don't do it Granda.

TOMMY   What?

WAYNE   You know... on the waltzer...

TOMMY   Aa love rock and roll! Ya Granny hates it. Ah'm th'
oldest rocker in Jarra! Ye should have seen us with me drape and blue suede
shoes!

Tommy sings, 'Blue Suede Shoes.'

> Well it's one for the money
> Two for the show
> Three to get ready
> Now go cat go
> But you don't step on my blue suede shoes
> You can do anything but lay off blue suede shoes.
> Blue... blue... blue...

WAYNE   *Pulling on Tommy's sleeve.*
               Granda let's go to the dodgems!

Wayne and Tommy get into a dodgem car.

SFX: Dodgem cars. Wayne is driving.

TOMMY   *To Wayne.* Watch it Wayne! Gan canny.

WAYNE   I love driving Granda.

SFX: Dodgems crashing.

WAYNE   An' crashing!

TOMMY   *Looking up as dodgem slows down.*
               Aa'll have ti' have aa lie doon. Do ye want ti go on th'
waltzer again?

WAYNE   No Granda! Let's go home.

Tommy and Wayne now.

TOMMY   Th' dog tried ti follow us home.

WAYNE   Can't remember the dog.

TOMMY   You only remember what you want to.
Indicating photographs. Aa've dug out aa few photos of when you wor
aa bairn.
Tommy hands photographs to Wayne.

WAYNE   *Indicating.* Me dad! Mam won't have a photograph of
him in the house.

TOMMY   She nevva forgave him.

WAYNE   Won't have his name mentioned.

TOMMY   Ya da wasn't aa bad bloke. Mind if any lass fluttered her
eye lashes at him he was away. He came ti see me after ya mam chased him.
She was right ti do it. Even he said that. She wanted nowt to do with him.
He kept saying, "I have ti make aa new life" over and over. Mind he'd had
aa canny drink. He wouldn't stay and fight for ye. It was easier ti go. Don't
ever walk away like ya da.

WAYNE   Tracey says you're my surrogate dad.

TOMMY   Sounds like aa medical experiment. Granda will do.

WAYNE   Granda.

TOMMY   Don't think ya anything like ya dad.

WAYNE   I not sure about that.

TOMMY   Ya not. Believe me. Aa'd take ye out for th' day, we'd go
down ti th' Pier, watch the fishermen just after aa'd retired and aa was
terrified ye'd get in with th' wrong crowd. You wa at that age, about
fourteen.

The Pier, South Shields, 1992.

SFX: The river.
*Wayne is 14, Tommy in his late 60's. They walk along the Pier, early
evening, watching the fishermen.*

WAYNE   *Indicating.* Why do the fishermen do it? Throw their
fishing lines in the sea, they can't see the fish, it's pitch black.

TOMMY   Aa've asked meself th' same question.

WAYNE   They never seem to catch anything.

TOMMY   Mebbe's it's ti get away from somethin.'

WAYNE   Their wives?

TOMMY   Ye might be right.

WAYNE   I wouldn't be like that.

TOMMY   Leave ya wife?

WAYNE   I'd stay with her... forever... that's what I'll do... like you
and Granny.

TOMMY   Ah'm glad ye feel like that.

WAYNE   I've never even had a Christmas card from dad... mam
says she'll never marry again... she said, "once was enough". It'll be enough
for me as well.

TOMMY   That's th' way aa felt, it's worked out for us. Aa was
lucky, aa got aa good wife, mind if ya Granny caught us looking at another
woman she'd kill us!

WAYNE   *Indicating.* He's caught something! I don't like to see
them wriggling like that. Are they still alive?

TOMMY   Til he knocks them on th' heed!
Looking at Wayne who is now upset.
Ya daft bugga it's only aa fish!

Tommy and Wayne now.

TOMMY	Ye nevva liked to see them caught.

WAYNE   When that prisoner Habib would start his chanting again, I'd tell him, "Shut it! I'm stuck like you. We both are. Look at Dave. Not a care in the world. Doesn't worry. He just says, 'Do the job Wayne and pick up your wages'".
I can't do that. Why did Habib chant? To get away from things. Forget what's happening.

TOMMY	Aa know what ye mean.

WAYNE	Do you?

TOMMY	Aa did things aa'll nevvor forget.

WAYNE	I can't.

TOMMY	Aa knaa.

WAYNE	Flashbacks.

TOMMY	Sweaty dreams.

WAYNE	Do they ever go?

TOMMY	Sometimes ye forget ti remember.

WAYNE	But you still remember?

TOMMY   Ya Granny used ti say, "Tommy, ya half-elephant, half-man! And I'm not sure about th' man bit".

WAYNE   It's not a bloody joke! Will you listen for once in your life.

TOMMY	Aa do listen it's just sometimes aa don't hear.

WAYNE	This is killing me.

TOMMY	Aa knaa th' feeling.

WAYNE   No you don't! I've got pictures burning in my head. I close my eyes and I see his face.

TOMMY   Ya not alone.

WAYNE   Listen! Would you take a pill to get the war out of your head? Stop you having those dreams.

TOMMY   When aa see mesel' crying on aa bunk with straw and lice for company and ah'm clammin wi' hunga, and aa wake up wi me fist in me mouth.

WAYNE   But would you take a pill?

TOMMY   Aa bloody box-full!

WAYNE   But we haven't! It doesn't stop other stupid shits doing it. Leaving all this. How do I get over it? A few drinks with me Granda and I'll be all right? That's nothing but shit!
Do you know why I was late tonight? Dave's mam rang... I had to go round to his... he'd locked himself in the bathroom... I had to break the door down... He'd cut his wrists.
I spewed everywhere.
He'd sent his mother to the town, gave her money, told her to spend it on herself. She wasn't away long. That's all he needed.
My last picture of Dave is him lying in a bath of blood.

End of Act One

Act Two

Holiday Camp, 1955

SFX'S: The camp tannoy plays a song of the day, which segues into an organ playing in the Ball Room.

WAYNE   *As Announcer.* Good evening campers! Will entrants for the knobbly knees competition please come to the Ball Room. Final call for the knobbly knees' competition. Don't be shy boys. The first prize is a week's holiday and the second prize, yes you've guessed it, two weeks! *Sotto Voce* Tomorrow evening ladies and gentleman we have a very special Gala Concert in the Regency Ballroom. It is the highlight of our Tenth Anniversary events commemorating the end of the War. 'Lest we forget.' And before I forget I have to say all you gorgeous ladies have been absolutely fantastic this week. We had a marvellous Beauty Competition round the pool today. The girls were stunning. In fact I jumped in the pool to cool myself down. It's a pity there wasn't any water in there! Only joking folks. And what can I say about last night's Glamorous Granny Final? Every one of them danced the Highland Fling on this very stage. It was something to behold. So gentlemen please do not let us down. In fact one of you lovely ladies out there has told me that her husband wants to enter the competition but that he's a little shy. I'm sure we can encourage him. *Out to audience.* Please give a warm round of applause to Mister Tommy Henderson. Yes I can see he is being a little shy. Let's give another round of applause to Mister Tommy Henderson.

Tommy enters slowly and gives a weak smile to the audience as he slowly rolls his trousers up to his knees.

Indicating to the audience. I see your wife's enjoying herself Mister Henderson and a little birdy tells me that you would like to give us a song.

TOMMY   That's very good of th' 'little birdy'.

WAYNE   *As Announcer to Tommy.* And I'm sure you'd love to sing a song before the knobbly knees competition gets underway. *To Audience.* Ladies and gentleman may I leave you in the very capable hands of Mister Tommy Henderson.

TOMMY   *Out to holiday camp audience.*
             Aa had ti be aa good singer at home because we nevva
had aa lock on our lavvy door. *Pauses, looks out, hopefully.*
Aa remember singing this for me mates during th' war. Aa'll never forget
them. This is for th' lads that didn't survive.

*Tommy sings, **We'll Meet Again**.*

We'll meet again, don't know where, don't know when
But I know we'll meet again some sunny day
Keep smiling through, just like you always do
Till the blue skies chase the dark clouds far away...

Tommy breaks off from song, becoming upset.

Tommy and Wayne now.

WAYNE   Dave's mam couldn't stop crying. His dad never said a
word. Sat dead still on the settee but then he started. Never heard a man cry
like that. When the ambulance came they wouldn't let Dave go, hung onto
him. His dad's shirt was covered in blood. After they took him away there
was just silence. His mam and dad cuddling Dave's photograph, looking at
me and I knew what they were thinking.

TOMMY   "It should have been you"? You're not ti blame.

WAYNE   I bloody know!

TOMMY   Ah'm struggling here.

WAYNE   It's not about you!

TOMMY   But it's about us.

WAYNE   'Us?' I don't want this shite. I've had enough. I could
end up like Dave.

TOMMY   Don't even think like that! Aa mean it. Aa'd bloody
morder ye if ya did anything! So help me aa would.

WAYNE	More bloody jokes.

TOMMY	It's not aa joke and aa know it.

Tommy slowly takes a photograph from an envelope.

WAYNE	I've never seen him before.

TOMMY   Ye wouldn't. It's John Anderson. Lovely lad. Dead posh
and dead nervous. He'd sit beside me but nevva said aa word for ages, then
he started: where he lived, his family. He was going ti' university when he
got home. Th' family had money.
Aa caught him one night breaking his heart. He couldn't stand it any more.
Aa said aa'd look after him. Do anything for him. Ye had to fight t' live. He
didn't. He lost heart. No wonder. Heads shaven, our own mothers wouldn't
have recognised us.
Aa wish aa hadn't done it! Ye've got me going over all sorts of things.
In th' camp there was hundreds of Polish soldiers, arms and legs missing.
Their own cavalry had charged th' German tanks. They'd been fed on
propaganda. It broke John's heart looking at them. When he found out his
brother had been killed he went berserk. We had ti hold him down. He was
going ti have aa go at th' guards. He broke down. Aa carried him to his
bunk.

German POW Camp, 1943.

Tommy and Wayne, as John, late evening.

WAYNE   *As John.* I can't stand it any more Tommy. I loved my
brother. I'm losing everything.

TOMMY	We'll beat th' bastards, mark my words.

WAYNE	*As John, through his tears.* Tommy. I've had enough. I can't go on.

TOMMY	Howay John ye can make it.

WAYNE	*As John.* Your voice is telling a different story.

TOMMY   Wa in this together.

WAYNE   *As John.* Not for much longer. I want out. I'm going to
die.

TOMMY   It's just th' way ya feeling...

WAYNE   *As John.* It's every minute, each day... take this...
John produces a blade.

TOMMY   Where'd ye get this?

WAYNE   *As John.* It doesn't matter. Use it ... cut my wrists... I'll
just lie here... drift away... I can't take any more...

TOMMY   Aa can't...

WAYNE   *As John.* It's either that or have the guards beat me up
when I refuse to work...

TOMMY   Th' take pleasure in doin' that: th' bastards!

WAYNE   *As John.* Come on Tommy... for me...

TOMMY   It's too much ti ask. How will aa live with it?

WAYNE   *As John.* You said you'd look after me...
He takes Tommy's hand.

TOMMY   How will aa forget?

WAYNE   *As John.* By remembering it's what I wanted. ... I've tried
to do it myself... failed... don't fail me and never blame yourself...

*Tommy looks at John for sometime, Wayne, as John, presents his arms to
Tommy who cuts John's wrists.*

Tommy and Wayne now.

WAYNE   You helped him kill himself.

TOMMY   And even my mate Geordie didn't know. We helped ti bury him... it pissed down wi' rain... suppose it had to...
We sang 'Abide With Me.' Aa cried and cried. Th' army's right ye knaa, th' giv' ya "travel, excitement..."

WAYNE   Then get your arse shot off! I was the only one in that Land Rover without a scratch. Except for the stuff in my head. That's what the army's given me.

TOMMY   Ye've still got ti keep goin'.

WAYNE   Who says? Dave tried and look how he ended up.

TOMMY   Dave had nowt ti live for, you've got aa lovelee son, aa lass that loves you and she's already put up with aa lot.
Aa've seen your bairn, somethin' ya Granny nevva had th' chance of doing. Harry's aa lovely little lad and ye making aa great da.
Tracey, ya bairn, even ya mother, look ti you. You've got ti be there for them. Especially when ah'm not around any more.

WAYNE   What you saying? I need you.

TOMMY   Aa'll be here as long as aa can.

WAYNE   Don't talk like that.

TOMMY   You'll survive without me. Aa've survived on scraps: Red Cross parcels; aa few fresh vegetables, bread from th' Poles. When th' had us working on th' farms, ah'd barter: cigarettes in exchange for veg. Aa'd wrap th' cigarettes in paper an' hide them in cow shit. Ye can't imagine smoking them after that! But aa did.

WAYNE   The lads say, "It's a just a job, that's the end of it." But it wasn't for you and it's not for us. You never think when you sign-up...

TOMMY   Two days after your eighteenth...

Working Man's Club, 1996.

Wayne and Tommy in working man's club: Wayne's eighteenth birthday.

TOMMY   *Out to the bar.* He's eighteen today.

WAYNE   *Looking round, then to Tommy.*
               I've been drinking in here for a year.

TOMMY   But it's ya forst legal drink! Where ya going later?

WAYNE   Me and ... Tracey are having a meal.

TOMMY   'Tracey?'

WAYNE   We've been going out two months on Tuesday.

TOMMY   As long as she's aa canny lass. Mind ya mam and
Granny'll have to inspect hor: family tree... criminal record... th' usual.

WAYNE   Never?

TOMMY   Aa was th' same with ya mam. Not that it did much
good. My da was worse with me sister's boyfriends' had ti have her back in
th' house before ten or th' was hell on. He was strict. Good bloke. Straight
as aa dye. He was in th' East Yorkshire Regiment in th' First World War.
Fought at Gallipoli, had frostbite and dysentery. That's when ye've got th'
shi... Aa've got something for ye now you're eighteen and aa bit more
sensible.
Tommy hands metal case to Wayne.
Aa want ye ti guard them with ya life.

WAYNE   Your dad's medals! I've looked at them loads of times.

TOMMY   Have ye now? Me Dad giv them ti me before th' war...

WAYNE   Before you signed-up. Joining the army has got to be
better than stacking shelves in a supermarket.

TOMMY   Aa'd like ye ti have them and ye'll get mine when aa pop
me clogs but that'll not be for aa while!

WAYNE   Like a family tradition.

TOMMY   *Indicating to the bar.* De ye knaa how ti gan on at th'
bar?

WAYNE   What do you mean?

TOMMY   About buying aa bloody round!

WAYNE   *Indicating medals.*
               This means a lot to me. I'll show them to Tracey....

TOMMY   Mine's aa bottle of Brown. And whatever ye want for
yoursel'.

WAYNE   *Looking closely at the medals.* Great.

Tommy and Wayne now.

Tommy showing Wayne a photograph.

TOMMY   These lads joined-up wi' me. How many are alive?

WAYNE   Granda!

TOMMY   None of th' buggas! It's th' one thing aa can't dodge.
Aa haven't got as far ti go, th' Crem's only down th' road.

WAYNE   Granda!

TOMMY   *Indicating envelope.* Aa've written what aa want.

WAYNE   What you on about?

TOMMY   Ah'm putting me house in order.

Tommy hands Wayne the envelope.

WAYNE   What is it?

TOMMY   Ya instructions. Ya Granny didn't want ti be buried. Sh'
said, when she was dying, that she'd feel funny with me lying with my back
ti her!

TOMMY   *Indicating.* Her ashes are in th' sideboard. Keep us
together. There's enough money ti buy plenty of drink at th' do, after th'
Crem. Aa don't want anything religious, not after what aa've been through.
But aa do want ye ti play 'Blue Suede Shoes' when everybody's walking out
and play it bloody loud!

WAYNE   *In tears.* I don't want this.

TOMMY   Ah'm not keen mesel. But as ya Granny used t' say,
"Once ya twenty-one th' years fly by". And th' hav. And they did. What
happened ti that big boozy bugger that used to come home on leave?
Throwing his weight about.

WAYNE   I know what you're going to say. It was only once.

TOMMY   Ya mam rang ti tell us ye were on your way round here.

WAYNE   *Walking away from Tommy.*
            I was half-cut...thought I knew it all because I'd done
well in training at Aldershot, been to Germany, Northern Ireland twice. I still
knew nothing.

TOMMY   Ye started as soon as you came through th' door just as
well ya Granny was at th' bingo.

Tommy's home, 1998.

Wayne, now twenty, walks toward Tommy.

WAYNE   Mam says you're going to sort me out!

TOMMY   If that's what it takes.

WAYNE   It'll take a bigger man than you…Granda…old man! I bring a few of me squaddie mates' home, and it's a big deal when I fall over the coffee table. I told mam I'll buy a new one. Buy two! That's not good enough.

TOMMY   Can ye not see what ya doing?

WAYNE   I'm doing nowt. Actually you don't know what I'm doing! No one asks me about the army! I came near the top in training. You don't want to know. Nobody does.

TOMMY   Aa have asked how ya doing! All aa get is aa grunt. Or you're too full of drink aal th' time you're home on leave.

WAYNE   They respect me in the army. Do you?

TOMMY   Ye earn respect.

WAYNE   You'll wish you'd never said that.

TOMMY   Doesn't stop it being true.

Wayne moves toward Tommy aggressively.

WAYNE   I'll batter you.

TOMMY   Give it ya best shot bonny lad.

Tommy and Wayne now.

WAYNE   I woke up half-dead. *Indicating.* On this settee.

TOMMY   Ye said sorry and that was enough. Aa made ye aa cup of tea and aa nevva said a word ti ye Granny when she came in from th' bingo. Or your mam. It'll always be our secret.

WAYNE   *Wayne picks up Tommy's letter.*
               I'll do everything in this letter Granda, I'll make sure your 'do' is great. The best ever in the club. I'll not let you down.

TOMMY   I know you'll not. You never have.

WAYNE   We shouldn't be in Iraq. I know it's our job to be there. I
said it to that prisoner Habib. Then he comes out with it. In perfect English,
" I agree with you".

TOMMY   He spoke English? That was aa turn up for th' books!

WAYNE   Studied in England. Got a degree and a teaching job in a
university. Just before the war broke out he went home to Baghdad.
He said he had nothing to do with Al-Qaeda. But when people see his
dishdasha he's guilty. He wanted out. We'd been stuck together for months
and finally we had something in common.

TOMMY   Why'd he take so long ti speak?

WAYNE   He had to be sure he could trust me. He said we were
both prisoners. I was a working class man and a victim in an unjust war....
bullshit! It was my choice to join the army. I knew I could be killed. I could
see what he was trying to do.

TOMMY   What was that?

WAYNE   Get me to see his point-of-view.

TOMMY   Was that wrong?

Wayne does not reply.

TOMMY   Did ye not get aa shock when he spoke English?
It would hav' been like my mate Geordie speaking Swahili. He could only
just manage English! Aa loved th' daft bugger. We wor together right until
th' end of th' war.

German POW Camp, Summer 1944.
Tommy and Wayne, as Geordie.

WAYNE   *As Geordie, looking at his arms and legs.*
Tommy there's sum heat in that sun. Aa'll get aa tan. Wi
could be on th' beach at Shields.

TOMMY	Aye wi' th' guards and guns and twenty feet high fence.
WAYNE reet?	*As Geordie.* Ye've got aa point there Tommy. Are ye all
TOMMY	"Aal reet!" Nah. Ah'm too bloody hot!
WAYNE	*As Geordie.* De ye knaa wot day it is?
TOMMY	Nae idea.
WAYNE	*As Geordie.* Durham Miners' Gala.
TOMMY	Nevva!
WAYNE	*As Geordie, looking up at the sky.* Mind they've got aa lovely day forrit.
TOMMY	Is that aa joke?
WAYNE	*As Geordie.* Ah'm just saying...
TOMMY Geordie.	Aa could cry mesel ti sleep! Ah'm stuck with aa daft
WAYNE	*As Geordie.* Who's that Tommy?
TOMMY God Almighty!	Ah'm struggling heor Geordie! Giv it aa break.
WAYNE every neet.	*As Geordie.* Aa knaa, ah'm th' same, aa've been prayin'
TOMMY	Aa need more than prayers.
WAYNE *prayer.*	*As Geordie, kneeling and bringing his hands together in* Bless me Father for I have sinned...
TOMMY	That's what ye say at Confession!

WAYNE   *As Geordie.* Aa couldn't think of any other prayers.

TOMMY   Say what's in yer heart. Some bugga might listen.

WAYNE   *As Geordie, pauses, for sometime.*
               God pin back ya lugs an' listen ti two Geordies in aa lot
of bother, me and me marrer are struggling, giv wi aa hand, get wi out of
here and aa promise….

TOMMY   Nae promises!

WAYNE   *As Geordie.* God, 'nae promises', but still help us!

TOMMY   That was reet from th' heart, let's hope he had his
hearing aid in. Ya aa funny bugger Geordie. Go on and tell us some of ya
daft jokes.

WAYNE   *As Geordie, in performance mode.*
               Geordie said to his mate, "Aa'll see ye at th' bottom of
th' street. If aa get there first aa'll put aa cross on th' ground, if you get there
forst rub it out."

Tommy and Wayne now.

TOMMY   Geordie wasn't th' brightest but he got me through many
aa bad day.

WAYNE   Dave was the same, he'd tell a daft story and have you
laughing. I needed that.

TOMMY   One thing aa lornt: live each minute. Five years in th'
camps taught me that. Aa once worked it out, it's about two and aa half
million minutes!
As time went on, th' guards changed, there was more and more owld men,
cos th' young ones had ti fight at th' front. Germany was retreating.
That's when Geordie and me wor sent to another farm, it was th' back end of
th' summer, 1944, wi worked for Herr Pisk.

TOMMY   Geordie loved working in th' open. Aa'd never seen him so happy, since we'd been captured. Herr Pisk had four sons in th' German army. He could speak English but he was quiet this day. We wor standing for ages just looking at the farm.

German Farm, late summer, 1944.

TOMMY   Herr Pisk…it is…aa good day.

WAYNE   *As Herr Pisk.* Bad day Tommy.

TOMMY   Th' sun is shining! Th' farm looks beautiful. You have aa lovely wife.

WAYNE   *As Herr Pisk.* My sons are not here. Home never the same Tommy. Two of my sons have been killed…a father should not have to bury his sons.

Tommy and Wayne now.

TOMMY   He looked ti th' farmhouse, his eyes filled-up. Then he pulled aa big blue hankie out of his pocket an' started ti cry.
Aa didn't want to but aa couldn't help mesel. Aa thought of his grief, even after what th' Germans had done ti us. Aal th' minutes he'd hav' ti' count without two of his sons, aa felt for him, he wasn't ti' blame for what happened ti me and Geordie.

WAYNE   Did you see much of Geordie after the war?

TOMMY   He married aa lass from Shields. That was th' last aa saw of him. Christmas cards. Th' odd phone call. He rang when his wife died. Aa went to th' funeral and then ti' his six months later.
Aa heard he was aa heavy drinker and knocked his wife about, aa don't knaa if that was because of th' war, it couldn't have helped. It gets us aal in different ways.

WAYNE   I have this nightmare, the Land Rover's just gone up in flames and it's me that's burning in the fire. Dave's saying, "you'll make it, come on Wayne". And I'm shouting, "It's not me Dave! It's you. It's not me".

TOMMY   Mebbe Geordie didn't want t' see me cos it was too
painful.

WAYNE   Geordie left you to cope with things on your own...

TOMMY   But aa had me family an' so have you...

WAYNE   Tracey wants me out the army and home in one piece,
she's said that ever since the bairn was born...

TOMMY   Aa'll never forget when ye came t' tell me,

WAYNE   I left the hospital and set off running. I was half way here
before I remembered. I'd come in my car!

TOMMY   Ye could hardly breathe.

WAYNE   I was screaming.

TOMMY   Aa thought something was wrong.

WAYNE   I'd never seen anything so lovely. The most beautiful
skinned rabbit in the world. I was a dad. You were a great grandfather.

TOMMY   Ya make me sound owld!

WAYNE   I was on top of the world!

TOMMY   Aa only wish ya Granny could have been there. And she
wouldn't want me crying. Ye've got th' son we never had...

WAYNE   You've had me.

Wayne, showing Tommy a photograph of Harry.

TOMMY   *Looking at photograph.* Harry's lovely.
Mind, aa've got ti say, he's th' double of me!

WAYNE   Everything was great, settled: Tracey, Harry, mam and you. I hardly ever thought about my dad, he was a distant memory. I wasn't bothered about seeing him; when I think about it I can't imagine how he could do it.

TOMMY   Write ye off?

WAYNE   I could never do that to Harry. But then I was back. Another tour of duty, second time in Iraq. End of story. In the prison I showed Habib photographs and talked about my home and family, he told me about his life and his country's history.
How Iraq invented irrigation, produced their own food twelve thousand years ago and a legal system five thousand years ago, but when we see the colour of his skin and robes, we think he's a terrorist.

TOMMY   He's right there.

WAYNE   What do the Shias and Sunnis mean to us? There were a thousand bodies a week in the mortuary in Baghdad alone. No one knows how many have died in Iraq. Habib's father was killed. A single bullet in his head, 'an execution killing'. That's what it's called.
I began to see his life: country attacked, family in danger, father killed. At the beginning of the war I thought we were getting rid of an evil ruler but what were we giving them? Should we have been there? I asked myself questions. I was seeing it from his point of view.
I told Dave that I wanted to help Habib to escape.

TOMMY   Bloody hell!

WAYNE   He thought I was crackers.
I told him about Habib, his family, how he had lived in England, even mentioned a bit about Iraq's history but not too much, I knew Dave wouldn't be that interested.

TOMMY   Ye wor probably right there.

WAYNE   We didn't talk about it again and then a couple of days later he just walked straight up to me and goes, "Let's do it. I'd do anything for you mate. I'll not let you down."

TOMMY   Bloody hell Wayne!

WAYNE   Dave got a uniform for Habib and a security pass. Don't
ask how. He had this plan: set-up a diversion and we did.

TOMMY   You and Dave wor risking everything

WAYNE   Habib said, "Look at Habib's uniform. I am a British
soldier. And tonight I will sleep with my friends, they will take a risk to have
me under their roof."

TOMMY   Aa don't knaa if aa want ti hear any more.

WAYNE   Then he said, "You will get your reward in Heaven. Like
me. "Wa alikum salaam. And God be with you." We watched him disappear
into the night.

TOMMY   There must have been hell on.

WAYNE   I kept thinking about what Habib had said.

TOMMY   Where was ya security?

WAYNE   "You will get your reward in Heaven. Like me."

TOMMY   Was the place not swarming?

WAYNE   Luck was on our side. The Prison was attacked that night.
All the security systems were hit. No CCTV. Complete blackout. Everything
dead.

TOMMY   Ye've been lucky? Ye could have been court-marshalled.
Done time in prison. It's treason. Th' could throw the bloody book at ye.
Bloody hell aa can hardly believe what ya saying. It doesn't bear thinking
about. Bloody hell.

WAYNE   I thought I'd done the right thing. It seemed wrong him
being trapped. I gave him a chance. Helped him to get home to his family.
Let him pray in peace. That's what Dave and me lived with.

TOMMY	Helping him ti escape?

WAYNE	Now it's just me that's got to live with that fear of being

caught.

TOMMY	And aa've gone sixty years living with what aa didn't do.

At th' back end of 1944, th said th' war'll be over soon. Th' prison guards
wor terrified th' Russians would liberate th' camp. They'd heard stories of
what they'd done ti other German guards. One of them, Schmidt, got aa hold
of me.

German POW Camp, end of 1944.

Wayne as German prison guard, Schmidt.

WAYNE	*As Schmidt* Henderson... I have a family... five

children... with a good wife and parents.

TOMMY	Why ya telling me?

Wayne, as Schmidt, hangs onto Tommy's arm.

WAYNE	*As Schmidt.* I do not want to die.

TOMMY	Aa knaaa th' feeling Herr Schmidt! It's too late ti' start

crying now.

WAYNE	*As Schmidt.* I would like for you to help me.

TOMMY	What can I do?

Wayne as Schmidt grabs Tommy.

WAYNE	*As Schmidt.* We could escape together.

TOMMY	Aa can't help ya.

WAYNE	*As Schmidt.* Please!

Tommy and Wayne now.

TOMMY   *To Wayne.* Aa still don't knaa what he expected me ti do or what aa should have done.

WAYNE   What happened?

TOMMY   Th' Russians liberated th' camp. Tore th' guards apart, limb-by-limb. Schmidt was one of them.

WAYNE   You could have saved him?

TOMMY   Who's ti blame? Th' man that makes th' gun or th' one that fires th' shot?

WAYNE   Like Dave and me.

TOMMY   For lettin' Habib go?

TOMMY   Ye did what ye thought was right, took th' law in ya own hands.

WAYNE   Were we responsible for his actions after that?

TOMMY   Nah.

WAYNE   If Habib commits a crime are we to blame?

TOMMY   What ya trying ti say?

WAYNE   Habib had told me about Iraqi history and the reasons why the West was attacking his country. I kept going over what Habib said, "You will get your reward in Heaven. Like me".

TOMMY   And?

WAYNE   I'd use the Internet at the American base to email Tracey. There was a story about Baghdad on CNN, and a link to an Arabic station I followed it and there was a video of a suicide bomber. It was Habib!
He was saying, "This video is to my family, and for all Iraqis who have been tortured and killed in their thousands by the Allied Forces.

WAYNE   I am going to heaven soon. Allah will bless my mission, purify my soul so that I am fit to see him. I long to be with my father and my brothers in arms who are already with him. This is the happiest day of my life. I am ready to die now. The oppressors must be overcome. I pray many die with me!"

TOMMY   Bloody hell Wayne!

WAYNE   Habib was a bright bloke, knew his politics and history, made it come alive. How could he want to end his life? He was married, had children, a family like me and Tracey and Harry. I felt near to him. I trusted him. Bigger fool me. Some of our lads, on principle, wouldn't trust any bugger. We did. How could he do that to Dave and me? We risked everything. He used us, treated us like shit. That's what trust does for you. He was walking toward a police station. The bomb went off too early. He was killed, some people were injured, but no one, apart from Habib, died. He said it was the happiest day of his life. We did what we thought was right. And we were terrified we'd get caught, but nothing happened, except all this stuff in my head.

TOMMY   Ah'm still waiting for my war in me heed ti die. At th' end of 1944 Geordie and me managed ti get out th' camp. It was freezing. British planes wor bombing Germany ti bits.
We headed for Berlin and got aa lift off some Americans in th' back of their truck. It was Christmas Eve. We wor frozen ti th' bone singing 'Silent Night'. One of th' Americans said, "If that don't make you cry, nothing will." Geordie bubbled like aa bairn. So did aa.

WAYNE   Where'd you end up?

TOMMY   An American camp in Berlin. Th' de-loused us and we wor interrogated by th' War Crimes Commission, ye had ti name Germans that had mistreated us.

WAYNE   You told them about 'Scarface?'

TOMMY   By hell aa did! For what he did ti th' Jewish lad. We got aa American plane back ti England. That was th' forst time aa'd ever flown! Then aa train ti Newcastle on New Year's Eve. Aa can see th' station now, thousands there. Th' crowd started singing 'Auld Lang Syne'
Picks up the letter from the hospital.
You know what I was saying about me instructions for when aa die.

WAYNE   Give me a break. I can't take any more.

TOMMY   Hav' ye noticed how nobody says 'dies'. When ya looking at th' 'Deaths' in th' paper. It's always, "slipped away peacefully."

WAYNE   And?

TOMMY   Aa saw th' consultant. Nice fella. Lovely smile. Mind he was very softly `spoken. Aa didn't hear aa word he said. When aa was leaving, th' receptionist asked if aa wanted aa copy of th' consultants notes sent home? Aa said aye.
Aa got th' letter yesterday. *Indicating letter.* Aa knaa it's bad news. Aa've had enough of that in me time. Mind aa've had aa good innings. You'll hav' ti open it. *Hands letter to Wayne.*

WAYNE   *Wayne opens letter* It's benign.

TOMMY   Aa knew it! It's just as well aa've got me bag packed for th' hospital in th' sideboard.

WAYNE   It means it's not malignant. You've got the all clear.

TOMMY   Are ye sure? Bloody hell! Aa thought ye meant, "there's not much time!"

WAYNE   You daft old bugger!

TOMMY   Not so much of th' daft!

WAYNE   Now you've got more time.

TOMMY   No, you and me have! It's aa reprieve for me. Like extra time after aa draw.

WAYNE   What you going on about?

TOMMY   Th' hospital's given me th' 'all clear' but aa can't live forever. I'm going ti die and it'll be sooner not later.

WAYNE   Don't...

TOMMY   Make th' most of us.

WAYNE   I will.

TOMMY   And do what aa asked ye ti do in th' instructions. That's what aa want. What about you?

WAYNE   I want out the army. What we did for Habib was bad enough to handle when Dave was alive but now I'll be waiting for somebody to tap me on the shoulder. When Dave was there it helped.

TOMMY   Th' poor lad can't say nowt ti no bugger.

WAYNE   He can in my head. I close my eyes. I see Dave. I've got to carry this by myself.

TOMMY   Trust me ye don't! Ye've got your Granda. For th' time being anyway. De ye know ya Granny left aa few bob. It's just lying there.

WAYNE   In the bank?

TOMMY   Nah! In aa cardboard box in th' sideboard.

WAYNE   You're kidding?

TOMMY   Ye could buy yerself out. She'd love nothing better than ti help her grandbairn.

WAYNE   You can't do that now, you've got to put in a years
notice. I've still got to go back to Iraq.

TOMMY   Unless ye do what your Uncle Peter did.

WAYNE   Go AWOL?

TOMMY   Bloody hell what will aa do wi' ten thousand, four
hundred and twenty seven pounds? Ya Granny was always good wi' money,
it's amazing what ye can save out of ya pension.

WAYNE   Spend the bugger.

TOMMY   And aa'll tell ye what, let's get that bloody bottle of
champagne.

They exit together.
Music up.